My Prayer of Salvation

Father God, I am a sinner and need your forgiveness. I believe that Jesus Christ shed His precious blood and died for my sin. I am willing to change and turn from my sin. I now invite Jesus Christ to come into my heart and life as my personal Lord and Savior.

DATE: _____
(This is your new "Birth Day")
Congratulations! You are now born again!
HALLELUJAH!

Daily Prayer – by Apostle Melissa

Lord, You are Most High and worthy to be praised! I renounce all thoughts and activities that oppose Your existence, Your authority, and Your love. Please protect me, my family, and all that You have entrusted me with. Bring forth my Divine connections, Divine relationships, Divine open doors of opportunity, Divine healing, Divine resources and Divine favor. Lord, bless my enemies and all of those who have spitefully misused me. They need You more than they know! Please forgive me for anything I've done that grieves You. Please teach me to honor and obey Your Word and to hear Your voice. In Jesus' name I pray. Amen.

My Prayer

TODAY'S DATE: _____

✝ **TODAY'S PRAYER FOCUS IS:**

✝ **PEOPLE I AM PRAYING FOR:**

THREE THINGS I'M GRATEFUL FOR TODAY:

♥ **RECORD "GOD RESPONSES" HERE. WHAT IS HE SAYING TO YOU ABOUT WHAT YOU ARE PRAYING FOR?**

Psalm 23:3

He refreshes and restores my soul (life); He leads me in the paths of righteousness for His name's sake.

My Prayer

TODAY'S DATE: _____

✝ **TODAY'S PRAYER FOCUS IS:**

✝ **PEOPLE I AM PRAYING FOR:**

THREE THINGS I'M GRATEFUL FOR TODAY:

♥ **RECORD "GOD RESPONSES" HERE. WHAT IS HE SAYING TO YOU ABOUT WHAT YOU ARE PRAYING FOR?**

Mark 11:25

And whenever I stand praying, if I have anything against anyone, I will forgive him and let it drop (leave it, let it go), in order that my Father Who is in heaven may also forgive me and my [own] failings and shortcomings and let them drop.

My Prayer

TODAY'S DATE: _____

✞ **TODAY'S PRAYER FOCUS IS:**

✞ **PEOPLE I AM PRAYING FOR:**

THREE THINGS I'M GRATEFUL FOR TODAY:

♥ **RECORD "GOD RESPONSES" HERE. WHAT IS HE SAYING TO YOU ABOUT WHAT YOU ARE PRAYING FOR?**

1 Peter 3:9

I will never return evil for evil or insult for insult (scolding, tongue-lashing, berating), but on the contrary blessing [praying for others welfare, happiness, and protection, and truly pitying and loving them].

My Prayer

TODAY'S DATE: _____

✝ **TODAY'S PRAYER FOCUS IS:**

✝ **PEOPLE I AM PRAYING FOR:**

THREE THINGS I'M GRATEFUL FOR TODAY:

♥ **RECORD "GOD RESPONSES" HERE. WHAT IS HE SAYING TO YOU ABOUT WHAT YOU ARE PRAYING FOR?**

Isaiah 58:8

Then shall my light break forth like the morning, and my healing (my restoration and the power of a new life) shall spring forth speedily.

My Prayer

TODAY'S DATE: _____

✝ **TODAY'S PRAYER FOCUS IS:**

✝ **PEOPLE I AM PRAYING FOR:**

THREE THINGS I'M GRATEFUL FOR TODAY:

♥ **RECORD "GOD RESPONSES" HERE. WHAT IS HE SAYING TO YOU ABOUT WHAT YOU ARE PRAYING FOR?**

Isaiah 30:26

The Lord binds up my hurt and heals my wound.

My Prayer

TODAY'S DATE: _____

✝ **TODAY'S PRAYER FOCUS IS:**

✝ **PEOPLE I AM PRAYING FOR:**

THREE THINGS I'M GRATEFUL FOR TODAY:

♥ **RECORD "GOD RESPONSES" HERE. WHAT IS HE SAYING TO YOU ABOUT WHAT YOU ARE PRAYING FOR?**

Psalm 30:11

My God has turned my mourning into dancing for me; He has put off my sackcloth and girded me with gladness.

My Prayer

TODAY'S DATE: _____

✝ **TODAY'S PRAYER FOCUS IS:**

✝ **PEOPLE I AM PRAYING FOR:**

THREE THINGS I'M GRATEFUL FOR TODAY:

♥ **RECORD "GOD RESPONSES" HERE. WHAT IS HE SAYING TO YOU ABOUT WHAT YOU ARE PRAYING FOR?**

Psalm 31:7

I will be glad and rejoice in God's mercy and steadfast love, because He has seen my affliction, He has taken note of my life's distresses.

My Prayer

TODAY'S DATE: _____

✝ **TODAY'S PRAYER FOCUS IS:**

✝ **PEOPLE I AM PRAYING FOR:**

THREE THINGS I'M GRATEFUL FOR TODAY:

♥ **RECORD "GOD RESPONSES" HERE. WHAT IS HE SAYING TO YOU ABOUT WHAT YOU ARE PRAYING FOR?**

2 Corinthians. 1:3

Blessed be the God and Father of my Lord Jesus Christ, the Father of sympathy (pity of mercy) and the God [Who is my Source] of all comfort (consolation and encouragement).

My Prayer

TODAY'S DATE: _____

✝ **TODAY'S PRAYER FOCUS IS:**

✝ **PEOPLE I AM PRAYING FOR:**

THREE THINGS I'M GRATEFUL FOR TODAY:

♥ **RECORD "GOD RESPONSES" HERE. WHAT IS HE SAYING TO YOU ABOUT WHAT YOU ARE PRAYING FOR?**

Psalm 147:3

You, Lord, heal my broken heart and bind up my wounds [curing my pains and my sorrows].

My Prayer

TODAY'S DATE: _____

✝ **TODAY'S PRAYER FOCUS IS:**

✝ **PEOPLE I AM PRAYING FOR:**

THREE THINGS I'M GRATEFUL FOR TODAY:

♥ **RECORD "GOD RESPONSES" HERE. WHAT IS HE SAYING TO YOU ABOUT WHAT YOU ARE PRAYING FOR?**

Psalm 107:20

You send forth Your word and heal me and rescue me from the pit and destruction.

My Prayer

TODAY'S DATE: _____

✝ **TODAY'S PRAYER FOCUS IS:**

✝ **PEOPLE I AM PRAYING FOR:**

THREE THINGS I'M GRATEFUL FOR TODAY:

♥ **RECORD "GOD RESPONSES" HERE. WHAT IS HE SAYING TO YOU ABOUT WHAT YOU ARE PRAYING FOR?**

Luke 6:28

I will invoke blessings upon and pray for the happiness of those who curse me, I will implore God's blessing (favor) upon those who abuse me [who revile, reproach, disparage, and high handedly misuse me].

My Prayer

TODAY'S DATE: _____

✝ **TODAY'S PRAYER FOCUS IS:**

✝ **PEOPLE I AM PRAYING FOR:**

THREE THINGS I'M GRATEFUL FOR TODAY:

♥ **RECORD "GOD RESPONSES" HERE. WHAT IS HE SAYING TO YOU ABOUT WHAT YOU ARE PRAYING FOR?**

Philippians 3:13

But one thing I do [it is my one aspiration]: forgetting what lies behind and straining forward to what lies ahead.

My Prayer

TODAY'S DATE: _____

✝ **TODAY'S PRAYER FOCUS IS:**

✝ **PEOPLE I AM PRAYING FOR:**

THREE THINGS I'M GRATEFUL FOR TODAY:

♥ **RECORD "GOD RESPONSES" HERE. WHAT IS HE SAYING TO YOU ABOUT WHAT YOU ARE PRAYING FOR?**

Luke 6:37

I will acquit and forgive and release (give up resentment, let it drop), and I will be acquitted and forgiven and released.

My Prayer

TODAY'S DATE: _____

✝ **TODAY'S PRAYER FOCUS IS:**

✝ **PEOPLE I AM PRAYING FOR:**

THREE THINGS I'M GRATEFUL FOR TODAY:

♥ **RECORD "GOD RESPONSES" HERE. WHAT IS HE SAYING TO YOU ABOUT WHAT YOU ARE PRAYING FOR?**

Psalm 30:2

O Lord my God, I cried to You and You have healed me.

My Prayer

TODAY'S DATE: _____

✝ **TODAY'S PRAYER FOCUS IS:**

✝ **PEOPLE I AM PRAYING FOR:**

THREE THINGS I'M GRATEFUL FOR TODAY:

♥ **RECORD "GOD RESPONSES" HERE. WHAT IS HE SAYING TO YOU ABOUT WHAT YOU ARE PRAYING FOR?**

Romans 8:37

In all things I am more than a conqueror.

My Prayer

TODAY'S DATE: _____

✠ **TODAY'S PRAYER FOCUS IS:**

✠ **PEOPLE I AM PRAYING FOR:**

THREE THINGS I'M GRATEFUL FOR TODAY:

♥ **RECORD "GOD RESPONSES" HERE. WHAT IS HE SAYING TO YOU ABOUT WHAT YOU ARE PRAYING FOR?**

Psalm 5:12

God's favor surrounds me like a shield. I have favor with God and men.

My Prayer

TODAY'S DATE: _____

✝ **TODAY'S PRAYER FOCUS IS:**

✝ **PEOPLE I AM PRAYING FOR:**

THREE THINGS I'M GRATEFUL FOR TODAY:

♥ **RECORD "GOD RESPONSES" HERE. WHAT IS HE SAYING TO YOU ABOUT WHAT YOU ARE PRAYING FOR?**

Romans 8:38,39

Nothing can separate me from the love of God.

My Prayer

TODAY'S DATE: _____

✝ **TODAY'S PRAYER FOCUS IS:**

✝ **PEOPLE I AM PRAYING FOR:**

THREE THINGS I'M GRATEFUL FOR TODAY:

♥ **RECORD "GOD RESPONSES" HERE. WHAT IS HE SAYING TO YOU ABOUT WHAT YOU ARE PRAYING FOR?**

Ephesians 1:4

God chose me in Him before the foundation of the world.

My Prayer

TODAY'S DATE: _____

✞ **TODAY'S PRAYER FOCUS IS:**

✞ **PEOPLE I AM PRAYING FOR:**

THREE THINGS I'M GRATEFUL FOR TODAY:

♥ **RECORD "GOD RESPONSES" HERE. WHAT IS HE SAYING TO YOU ABOUT WHAT YOU ARE PRAYING FOR?**

Proverbs 3:5

I trust in the Lord with all my heart and lean not to my own understanding.

My Prayer

TODAY'S DATE: _____

✝ **TODAY'S PRAYER FOCUS IS:**

✝ **PEOPLE I AM PRAYING FOR:**

THREE THINGS I'M GRATEFUL FOR TODAY:

♥ **RECORD "GOD RESPONSES" HERE. WHAT IS HE SAYING TO YOU ABOUT WHAT YOU ARE PRAYING FOR?**

Psalm 138:8

God is perfecting everything that concerns me.

My Prayer

TODAY'S DATE: _____

✝ **TODAY'S PRAYER FOCUS IS:**

✝ **PEOPLE I AM PRAYING FOR:**

THREE THINGS I'M GRATEFUL FOR TODAY:

♥ **RECORD "GOD RESPONSES" HERE. WHAT IS HE SAYING TO YOU ABOUT WHAT YOU ARE PRAYING FOR?**

Romans 8:28

God causes everything – even trials and setbacks – to work together for my good.

My Prayer

TODAY'S DATE: _____

✝ **TODAY'S PRAYER FOCUS IS:**

✝ **PEOPLE I AM PRAYING FOR:**

THREE THINGS I'M GRATEFUL FOR TODAY:

♥ **RECORD "GOD RESPONSES" HERE. WHAT IS HE SAYING TO YOU ABOUT WHAT YOU ARE PRAYING FOR?**

2 Corinthians 5:7

I walk by faith and not by sight.

My Prayer

TODAY'S DATE: _____

✝ **TODAY'S PRAYER FOCUS IS:**

✝ **PEOPLE I AM PRAYING FOR:**

THREE THINGS I'M GRATEFUL FOR TODAY:

♥ **RECORD "GOD RESPONSES" HERE. WHAT IS HE SAYING TO YOU ABOUT WHAT YOU ARE PRAYING FOR?**

Hebrews 6:12

It is by faith and patience that we inherit the promises of God, so I will exercise faith and patience.

My Prayer

TODAY'S DATE: _____

✝ **TODAY'S PRAYER FOCUS IS:**

✝ **PEOPLE I AM PRAYING FOR:**

1.
2.
3.
4.

THREE THINGS I'M GRATEFUL FOR TODAY:

1.
2.
3.

♥ **RECORD "GOD RESPONSES" HERE. WHAT IS HE SAYING TO YOU ABOUT WHAT YOU ARE PRAYING FOR?**

Isaiah 43:19

God is going to do a new thing in my life.

My Prayer

TODAY'S DATE: _____

✝ **TODAY'S PRAYER FOCUS IS:**

✝ **PEOPLE I AM PRAYING FOR:**

THREE THINGS I'M GRATEFUL FOR TODAY:

♥ **RECORD "GOD RESPONSES" HERE. WHAT IS HE SAYING TO YOU ABOUT WHAT YOU ARE PRAYING FOR?**

1 Corinthians 2:9

My eyes have not seen, nor my ears heard, nor has it even entered my heart all the wonderful things God has prepared for me.

My Prayer

TODAY'S DATE: _____

✞ **TODAY'S PRAYER FOCUS IS:**

✞ **PEOPLE I AM PRAYING FOR:**

THREE THINGS I'M GRATEFUL FOR TODAY:

♥ **RECORD "GOD RESPONSES" HERE. WHAT IS HE SAYING TO YOU ABOUT WHAT YOU ARE PRAYING FOR?**

Proverbs 17:22

A cheerful heart is good medicine, so I will laugh a lot, have lots of fun, be light-hearted, and enjoy my life.

My Prayer

TODAY'S DATE: _____

✝ **TODAY'S PRAYER FOCUS IS:**

✝ **PEOPLE I AM PRAYING FOR:**

THREE THINGS I'M GRATEFUL FOR TODAY:

♥ **RECORD "GOD RESPONSES" HERE. WHAT IS HE SAYING TO YOU ABOUT WHAT YOU ARE PRAYING FOR?**

1 John 2:20,27

I am anointed by the Lord. The anointing I received from Him abides in me permanently and teaches me concerning everything that is true.

My Prayer

TODAY'S DATE: _____

✞ **TODAY'S PRAYER FOCUS IS:**

✞ **PEOPLE I AM PRAYING FOR:**

THREE THINGS I'M GRATEFUL FOR TODAY:

♥ **RECORD "GOD RESPONSES" HERE. WHAT IS HE SAYING TO YOU ABOUT WHAT YOU ARE PRAYING FOR?**

Joshua 1:7

I am strong and very courageous and observe all of God's commands. I do not turn to the right or left, so I prosper wherever I go.

My Prayer

TODAY'S DATE: _____

✝ **TODAY'S PRAYER FOCUS IS:**

✝ **PEOPLE I AM PRAYING FOR:**

THREE THINGS I'M GRATEFUL FOR TODAY:

♥ **RECORD "GOD RESPONSES" HERE. WHAT IS HE SAYING TO YOU ABOUT WHAT YOU ARE PRAYING FOR?**

Galatians 6:9

I will not grow weary in doing good, for in due season I will reap a harvest if I faint not.

My Prayer

TODAY'S DATE: _____

✝ **TODAY'S PRAYER FOCUS IS:**

✝ **PEOPLE I AM PRAYING FOR:**

THREE THINGS I'M GRATEFUL FOR TODAY:

♥ **RECORD "GOD RESPONSES" HERE. WHAT IS HE SAYING TO YOU ABOUT WHAT YOU ARE PRAYING FOR?**

Isaiah 26:3

God will keep me in perfect peace because my mind is stayed on Him and I trust Him.

The Names of God

1. EL SHADDAI (LORD GOD ALMIGHTY)
2. EL ELYON (THE MOST HIGH GOD)
3. ADONAI (LORD, MASTER)
4. YAHWEH (LORD, JEHOVAH)
5. JEHOVAH NISSI (THE LORD MY BANNER)
6. JEHOVAH RAAH (THE LORD MY SHEPHERD)
7. JEHOVAH RAPHA (THE LORD THAT HEALS)
8. JEHOVAH SHAMMAH (THE LORD IS THERE)
9. JEHOVAH TSIDKENU (THE LORD OUR RIGHTEOUSNESS)
10. JEHOVAH MEKODDISHKEM (THE LORD WHO SANCTIFIES YOU)
11. EL OLAM (THE EVERLASTING GOD)
12. ELOHIM (GOD)
13. QANNA (JEALOUS)
14. JEHOVAH JIREH (THE LORD WILL PROVIDE)
15. JEHOVAH SHALOM (THE LORD IS PEACE)
16. JEHOVAH SABAOTH (THE LORD OF HOSTS)

Notes

Notes

Notes

Notes

Notes

Notes

Notes

Notes

Notes

Notes

Notes

John 10:10

Jesus came that we may have and enjoy life, and have it in abundance (to the full, overflowing) So, I will enjoy my life to the full and have abundance in every area - ministry, experiences, relationships, finances, and health.

www.ingramcontent.com/pod-product-compliance
Lightning Source LLC
Chambersburg PA
CBHW062006180426
43198CB00037B/2571